Camping
on the Wye

Camping
on the Wye

**The tale of a trip along the Wye
from Whitney in Herefordshire to Chepstow in 1892**

LOGASTON PRESS
Little Logaston, Logaston,
Woonton, Almeley, Herefordshire HR3 6QH

First published by Logaston Press 2003
Copyright © Michael Goffe 2003

ISBN 1 904396 06 2

Set in Garamond and Lucida and by Logaston Press
and printed in Great Britain by
The Cromwell Press

Preface

The original is a small leather bound, handwritten volume with the watercolour illustrations on a fairly thick cartridge paper with the text partly written thereon, but with the bulk of the text at the back of the book on a fine vellum. As the handwriting is not always easily decipherable a decisions was made to reset the text, the original being adhered to except where some clarification or additional punctuation made for happier interpretation. All but a few of the illustrations have been reproduced.

My thanks to Sarah Thredder who spent many hours deciphering the handwritten text and producing a text suitable for editing and subsequent publishing, and to her husband Phil for having the drive and enthusiasm to see the project come to fruition. Also to my wife Cate who has long thought that the book was of such merit that it deserved a wider readership than just my immediate family.

Introduction

The original sketch book and diary was given to me by my father, the E.G.L.G. or Gg. of the narrative, some 55 years ago. He was the last survivor of the four undergraduates of University College London who undertook their camping adventure in 1892. My father, Ernest George Leopold Goffe, could be descended from Willy Goffe, one of Oliver Cromwell's major-generals and one of those who signed Charles I's death warrant. Willy Goffe fled to America at the Restoration where he was pursued before disappearing from sight. Ernest Goffe was born in 1867 at Port Maria, Jamaica, the ninth son of a 'white Jamaican', owner of several estates producing originally sugar and latterly bananas, who also had interests in Port Maria, was a JP and a churchwarden. His mother, Margaret, was a lady described on her baptismal certificate as a 'mulatto' who by repute was a formidable person who ruled her household of children and servants with a firm hand, and tolerated her husband's many adventures as long as they were kept out of the family home. The elder sons of the marriage managed the different estates and later inherited them, while the three youngest children were sent to university abroad to finish their education and it was in this way that my father came to London University to study medicine at University College and Hospital. He was a great sportsman, playing rugby for UCH and also Rosslyn Park, besides hockey, badminton and golf.

The four taking part in the trip met as students at University College. C.G. (Dr. Charles Goring), like my father, was a medical student who, after qualifying, specialised in the diseases of the mind while my father went on to become a hospital doctor and, after marrying my mother in 1916, a GP in Kingston upon Thames. He retained his interest in boating, and especially sailing, all his life. C.G. died, I believe, before I was born, and his two sons became wards of my father and frequent visitors to our house. The elder, Donald, was killed in an aeroplane crash in Egypt in the 1930s, while his younger brother, Marius, became an actor of renown of stage screen and television.

Of A. Hair I know nothing, I can not remember his name ever being mentioned.

S.K. Baker was the main author and illustrator of the book. I remember being taken to his house in the 1930s by my father and being introduced. He was a bit of a shadowy figure and I believe remained a bachelor, but must have kept up his interest in boating as he was somewhat surprised and shocked that by the age of eleven I had not heard of or let alone read any of the Arthur Ransome books. He gave me his copy of *We did not mean to go to sea*, which I still have and remains my favourite of the series.

The 'Randan' skiff that they used on their journey down the Wye would have been about 28ft. long, with three rowing positions, one oar being used at the forward place, one on the opposite side at the rear place, with the middle seat using two sculls slightly shorter than the oars. It was a versatile set up and could also be rowed with different combinations of oars and oarsmen. At the end of the 19th and in the first half of the 20th century, similar and smaller skiffs were to be found in their hundreds, either privately owned or let out from the boatyards situated every few miles along the lengths of the non tidal Thames and other navigable rivers. Boating was a very popular pastime among all classes of society. It is of note that they did not choose a 'camping skiff', with metal hoops over the top supporting an all enveloping cover which served the double purpose of keeping out the rain and providing privacy and room to sleep, and incidentally the scenario for the downfall of many a maiden, as happened to the heroine in A.P. Herbert's novel, *Water Gypsies*.

Before the days of motor cars and boat carrying trailers, sending a boat by train was quite the normal thing. On our summer holiday in 1938, the family 14ft. sailing dinghy was pushed on a station trolley the half mile to Kingston Station, loaded into a goods waggon and a week later collected from Kingsbridge Station in south Devon, pushed to the quayside and sailed down to Salcombe. It was a method I had used as late as 1963 to transport a 9ft. dinghy, but nowadays there are no regular goods trains between stations, and no guards vans on trains.

I do not think it would be possible these days to hire a skiff to recreate this descent of the Wye, but it is a very popular canoeing river. Canoes may be hired easily and transported to any starting point and, except in times of flood, there are no real difficulties or dangers. Last year my wife and I canoed a short stretch and it was a memorable experience—a quiet easy flowing river, winding through lovely countryside with lots of interesting wildlife to be seen. I hope this book might give you the urge to explore the Wye for yourself—by boat of course.

Michael Goffe
September 2003

The Wye Tour

It wasn't until the middle of the 18th century that tourism in the British Isles became an acceptable form of relaxation and a new interest for the gentry. Antiquarians such as William Stukeley not only established a sense of history within the landscape, but also brought a realisation of the potential that buildings and ruins could have in becoming constituent parts of an idealised romantic landscape.

The appreciation of such landscapes 'in the raw' led to the 'tours' such as those in the Lake District, the Derbyshire Dales, and the Wye Valley becoming an acceptable alternative to 'taking the waters' at the growing spa towns.

The early tourists saw their voyages down the Wye as a sequence of scenic delights that included ruins such as Goodrich Castle and Tintern Abbey. They also saw beauty in the industrial developments in the form of the smoking iron furnaces that littered the riverside, the busy scenes of river traffic, and the commercial activities on the banks. The visual interest in such a tour is well described in the following:

> Immediately after passing under Wilton Bridge, we make acquaintance with the peculiarities of the Wye. Its 'winding bounds' are so remarkable that frequently after the boat has floated four or five miles we find ourselves within gun-shot of the place from which we started; a tree-clad hill, or a church-spire, seen directly in front, presently appearing at the side, or, in another moment, behind the spectator; while perhaps in a few minutes, it is immediately again in his onwards path: forming alternately a foreground or a background to the picture, and that so suddenly as to seem incomprehensible. On quitting the level land, the varied and broken scenery on either side suggests a vague though irresistible impression, that the craggy precipices, rocky ascents, and isolated plateaux, between which the stream takes its tortuous way‹now reposing in deep and glassy pools, then hurrying down a gushing rapid, as if 'behind time', and again stopping to take up at intervals the winding streamlets poured from receding elevations over the little greensward vales they encircle‹were the boundaries of a river always,‹in a word, that the Wye is a river designed by Nature itself.
>
> *The book of South Wales, the Wye and the Coast*, Mr. & Mrs. S.C. Hall, 1861

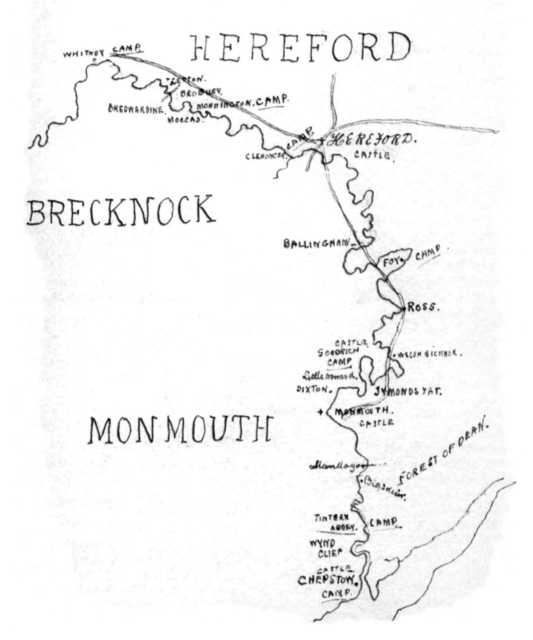

*The map that was drawn in the original sketch book
and which locates the camping sites mentioned*

Camping down the Wye

Plinlimmon, the mother of the river Wye, abounding in bogs and morasses, frequently shrouded in mists, and 2469 feet high sends forth from her springs and wells many a noble stream, foremost of which is the Severn, the Wye (150 miles long), the Rheidol, the Dulas etc. A notorious Welsh chieftain, named Owain Glyndwr made it his lair, and from its recesses descended on his forays to the Welsh Marches. At Rhayader the Wye loses its character of an impetuous mountain stream and becomes river-like with occasional shallows. In wet seasons it is navigable at Glasbury, fortunately for us the river of 1892 was a dry one, in fact was lower than for many years and our boat was launched at Whitney, a small village boasting of a railway station about 50 miles from the source.

Every part is attractive and the constant windings give ever changing views, becoming bolder and bolder as it nears its termination.

Earthworks of Roman and British origin, stones and crosses, castles and churches abound in the neighbourhood. Salmon and the usual kind of fish are plentiful. The speed of the current is about $5^{1}/_{2}$ miles an hour and the stream is about 10 feet below the alluvial surface. Otter hunting is still carried on in the more remote tributaries.

Geologists find the Silurian and Old Red Sandstone, inside some deposits of the Tertiary Period, and affirm that the river has been travelling through its rocky boundaries for no less than 1,274,000 years. Very ancient remains of the mammoth, cave bear, rhinoceros and human skeletons have been found in caves, notably those found at little Doward.

In Charles II's reign a sum of £1,300 was raised for the purpose of making the river navigable, traces of the work done may be seen at Monnington Weir etc. Some utilitarian soul proposed to supply London with Wye water to the amount of 393,000,000 gallons per day.

The reader may now wish to be introduced to our little party. It consisted of A. Hair—devoted to salmon fishing and photography, E.G.L.G.—an invaluable man on a camping trip, C.G.—of a philosophic turn of mind, and S.K.B.—a dabbler in art [often recorded as H. Gg., G. and B. in the following account].

It was H. who gathered to himself his friends, and armed with sundry guide books propounded unto them his views on a river camping trip. Jordan, boat builder of Hereford, supplied a Salter's Randan, and after much labour a Bell tent was secured and duly pitched in H.'s garden, its divided pole being admirably adapted for packing on board. Two rugs, waterproof sheets, tinned plates, mugs etc. and kit bags were indicated for each man, and a spirit cooking stove for three persons was secured. Groceries with the inevitable tinned meat were ordered to be ready at Paddington, not without protest from G. who had been living on canned provisions for a week on the Broads. Behold then a growler laden with tent, bundle of rugs, kit bags, three Gladstones and H. & Gg inside descending Haverstock Hill to meet G. and B. at the station on the evening of 12 August 1892.

B. somehow was late and left his luggage behind, came accompanied however by his banjo and a few spare hats. At Gloucester more luggage got astray and had to be wired for in several directions. We went on to Hereford and were duly met by Jordan. We secured beds and went through a settling of accounts in H.'s bedroom.

Hair's bedroom, Hereford—asking for settlement of preliminary expenses

Going down to the river in the morning we found two anxious looking gentlemen seated in an old boat waiting arrival of their canoes. Morning was spent visiting the Cathedral, buying stores and meeting trains for tidings of baggage, this eventually turning up we decided on losing no time in getting on to Whitney.

Last use of chairs, Hereford

Two porters conveyed our luggage across the city to another station, where we found the boat duly packed on a couple of trucks, our luggage filling a van and after some useful hints from Jordan we arrived in due course at Whitney. The train was somewhat delayed while our ample goods and chattels were deposited on the platform, a passenger throwing us an empty match box, no doubt thinking we had forgotten that useful item.

Photography at Barr's Court Station

View of Salter's Randan at Whitney and a few things to go into it

4

All the able bodied men in the village came round to assist in conveying us to the river and an imposing procession took place: G. in college blazer and B. with banjo, in the van, next the boat born on poles by men, then a cart with our baggage, H. & G. bringing up the rear. H. distributed ample largesse, and the boat gradually sank with our packing until it rested on the bottom, and much heaving was necessary to get her off.

5

We had not rowed far when we grounded again, a contingency
provided for by the rule that each man was to jump out
and either push or lift the boat.

Our first shoal: all hands overboard, water about 4 inches deep

After a mile or so we decided to camp and an elegant site was found nicely sheltered by the trees of a small copse. Unloading proceeded apace, the tent when put up attracting all the cows and horses in the field, water proofs were spread out and bags and baskets lugged inside, and we sat or laid down to await the boiling of the kettle.

Camp at Whitney

Trials of the amateur photographer! Hair finds after about 40 'snaps' that he has forgotten to have the shutter open

Tea over the strangeness of the thing came over us, but G. who has camped much (with the Volunteer Medical Service Corps) after a survey of the heavens disappeared with a spade and dug a trench all round. We disposed ourselves for sleep, two of the crew first warbling a few duets until G.'s snores drowned all else.

'The shades of night were falling fast - and H.'s pot <u>did</u> boil at last'

All snug

Early morn proved that G. sleeps with one eye open for seizing his air gun he rushed out

and

fired several

times into a

crowd of bovine visitors that were jostling each other to get inside the tent. A tiny thud, showing that he hast hit something, is followed by a lumbering trot and a general want of interest on the part of the animals. However, cows brought their calves to see us later on with pardonable feminine curiosity.

This roused us all and 'getting up' was suggested but nobody stired until B. found some beetles under his rug and got up without further ado. Soon four men variously attired were engaged in spreading rugs out to air, breakfast was set in order, and presently at a word from H. who had his camera ready, the others dived into the water from the boat with a mighty splash. Unfortunately this interesting scene, like one or two others of great interest didn't 'develop' as H. had forgotten his 'shutter'.

Ye small boy seeketh to inspire terror by ye Tale of Ye Mad Bulls

We discovered that we were near a path, and that the path lead to a house, from which house strolled the owner with not exactly an expression of welcome on his face. H. & G. who were in charge at the time artlessly tried weather topics and other things, but when the gentleman caught sight of G. & B. down the river, fishing, he mildly suggested that we 'might have asked leave'. However, satisfactory explanations ensued and later on he returned accompanied by a clergyman who, to the honour of his cloth, invited us to church and tea.

Now, some of us on a visit to the village had given heed unto the gossip of the place relating how a tent exactly like ours had been torn to pieces by cows, the owners perforce having to return to town sooner than they expected and as it had been established that where 'one of us went the others went too', we laid our bodily necessities before our spiritual and decided to stay in camp, thereby missing much that was delightful; for G. & B. strolling round the church in the evening saw a lovely vision of a fair damsel who was ascertained to be the vicar's daughter!

The transit of Venus & eclipse by the sun-shade

11

When night fell gusts of wind and rain shook our habitation, necessitating extra stays on the pole, and we lay quaking far into the night, as the animals were charging madly all about us, and at any time we might have entertained a stalled ox and hatred therewith.

To those who know not the pleasure of early rising, and there are a good many, a camping trip is to be commended. You wake and feel that you are truly one with nature. After that blissful half awake state succeeding a dreamless sleep, you throw off rugs and clad in flannels emerge directly into the sweet morning air warmed by the sun and laden with the promise of a lovely day. The grass stalks laden with dew, gently stirred by passing zephyrs love your feet, the birds welcome you the smoke and endless turmoil of the town is as a forgotten dream. With towels swinging you make for the bathing place and take an invigorating header into the pure cool water. The odour of frying bacon and eggs is then doubly grateful and the coffee delicious, boiling on a fire made of wood from the copse. Foaming fresh milk in abundance and marmalade wherewith to fill the crevices complete the meal. All sit round to discuss the morning pipe and plans for the day. Of course there are certain disagreeables, for instance when H. resignedly disappears with the crockery down to the water's edge and dabbles about in the mud to clear off the grease, we know as we sit and smoke that perhaps he does not take everything as cheerfully as he might. This general disinclination to 'wash up' may account for the gradual merging of one meal into the rest.

A shop in the village was found where bread, apples and oil were sold and we added a goodly supply to our store.

Furnace blast at Whitney

On Monday morning we struck tent and dropped down the hurrying river. Shallows bothered us somewhat at first and also the rapids, but by steering for the tongue of smooth water at the head of each fall we generally got through alright. Our feet and legs became sunburnt with exposure as we wore trousers turned up so as to be ready for emergencies. Sometimes the current would almost tear the boat out of our hands and when the others had got in the indefatigable G. would be hanging on desperately to the stern, then with a tremendous leap land on the top of bags, hats and general cargo, when the boat would plunge ahead, water seething all around and the stones at the bottom appearing to fly past. We stationed a man at the bow to fend her off going round corners as she had a nasty way of burying her nose in the bank, and his work was no sinecure as the bent pole often testified. At very awkward channels all got out and hung on until the best course was decided on. Occasionally jagged boulders would be seen, so close as to cause a shudder, and sometimes after a long scrunch we would 'get left' on the top of another, deep water all around into which G. once or twice boldly plunged, a veritable Jonah; a jab here and there usually sufficient to keep her right. Now comes a murmuring shoal right across the river and the good old boat would scrape along in a half hearted manner.

A well earned repast

Then comes a long quick reach, perhaps a leaping salmon alone breaking its placid surface. Just the place for lunch—and stroke dives into basket after bread and cheese. Lolling on seats and baggage all take a rest while the soothing weed sends up tiny cloudlets to join those above ... too soon another rapid demands attention, (the general impression on nearing a rapid is that it is approaching us like some great river dragon, whereas it is we who are being bourne rapidly by the stream into the midst of rushing shallows), or perhaps the guide book says something of interest is to be seen and we land to investigate. Afloat once more song resounds far down the stream, H. giving a verse of the Canadian boat song:-

Faintly as tolls the evening chime,
Our voices keep tune and our oars keep time
Soon as the words on the shore look dim
We'll sing of St. Anne's own parting hymn -
Row, brothers, row the stream runs fast
The rapids are near and the daylight's past

Now does Gg. try to secure game for the larder by shooting at rabbits which of course clear into holes on seeing the bullet, and now H. walks about in the boat casting the fly all round, 'though never a fish comes out to dine', whilst greatly disturbing the equilibrium of our craft.

Chorus of
'Ah! Ah'!

Gg. disgusted at rabbits seeks refuge in some mighty tome, while the jovial
G. describes himself as a 'simple country maiden with a beauty heavy laden',
or launching out into piratical sentiments sings out that 'once aboard the
lugger the girl is <u>mine</u>, and then?' 'Ah! Ah!' roar the crew in chorus, sending
some flapping heron miles down the river in disgust.
At Bredwardine a former student of the U.C.H. has set up for himself a
practice and a landing party is formed of G. & B., the latter somewhat
inconvenienced by a flapping rubber sole. However the place is under
repair and the deputation withdraws, and find H. & G. eating apples in an
orchard. G. is presented with a button hole of daisies by little girls at the
toll gate and they mulclt the rest of 1d. each.

Snags and shallows at Bredwardine

Easy all!

Easy all! Here Goring doeth a deed of daring,
and rescues two damsels in distress

Children scrambling for coppers. A boy having found one, stands by it, for the little girl to pick up.

The fall at Monnington

Once more we board the lugger, and soon a mighty fall is heard. We drift down cautiously and find a singular bed of flat sandstone rocks covering three fourths of the river, which confined on the left rushes through a narrow channel roaring over great boulders on either side.

This is rather a serious check and we pitch tent in a leafy dell facing the fall at sunset; a forage party visits a neighbouring farm for apples & milk; while G. climbs a tree the farmer's wife and B. receive the fruit. Heavy laden they return, a furnace having meanwhile been made in the bank. Lulled to sleep by the fall, snores resound from the tired voyagers.

Evening at Monnington Camp

'Stick to it G!' He does, and provides the camp with fresh water from the other side of the river. Good old G.

Morning, with the song of birds, finds us ready for breakfast but somewhat subdued by Gg. pointing out a decayed hedgehog floating in the pool from which he had drawn water over-night. Now G. & B. betake them to the boat which had got a nasty knock the previous day, and finding a hole rivet a strip of cedar over it. The luggage having been carried over the portage, the boat is towed round, held by a line from the stern to prevent her being drawn into the current. After hauling over rocks she takes the water below, and cargo being stowed we let go and quickly leave the fall. G. was with diffi-culty dissuaded from plunging through the fearful channel—fatal acci-dents had happened there, and we could not afford to loose our G.! The sun was high in the heavens when lunch was proposed, <u>and</u> carried up the bank to a flowery mead. A waterproof served for a table cloth, and the river received a choice collection of empty tins and pots.

We land at an inn, where G. obliges us with the 'polka and the choir boy', harmonium accompt.

Evening found us at the Monk's Boat House but seeing a ghostly advisor strolling round we decided on pitching on the opposite bank, so perpendicular as to necessitate hauling things up by ropes.

A dewy camp at Monk's Boat house near Hereford. Each has his allotted task — Goring makes a furnace in the bank, H. lugs things, Goffe with never-to-be-sufficiently-admired skill pitches the tent. B. tears down half a tree. The owner looks on.
'Here today and gone tomorrow?' remarked a woman passing in a boat. The welcome stew from Gg.'s pot put warmth into our souls and the duplex lamp the same thing for the tent. We lay around smoking and imbibing ale until one after another we fell asleep.

Hereford from the river

Next day saw us at Hereford and we landed for stores and some baggage which had arrived from London, changing oars for a pair of sculls, and purchasing river charts. Gg. & B. arrived from the market with arms and pockets laden and with welcome letters from the P.O. No time was lost in getting off and the Cathedral towers soon faded into the distance. More shoals and rapids, and the sculls began to show signs of wear for the turns were frequent and much poling necessary.

Going food foraging for provisions in Hereford,
not forgetting bunting (U.C.H. colours)

A lovely reach with banks crowned with trees, cattle standing knee deep in the stream watching us with 'slow bovine gaze' lashing each other's sides with tails, close packed the better to keep off flies, brought us to a lofty tree covered hill. At the angle of the river appeared a balloon tent, occupants seated outside with liquids on a table, smoking cigarettes, canoes hauled up on land. We hailed them & recognised canoeists from Hereford, having been about a week on that part of the journey.

'Nice evening, isn't it.'
'Very, going down?'
'Well, yes.
Staying
here
long?'

'Tomorrow.
See you
again.'
'Yes, ta ta.'
'Ta, ta.'

Dropping
down we
pulled up at
a field—
real steps
in the
bank the
better to
unload, borrowing
hedge stakes to support our pots and kettle over the fire. Now, supper being finished and all men weary the others slept while Gg. discoursed on philosophy, a stillness settled down over all things a lurid light filled the tent, and some creature gave a sharp cry, the earth trembled and the watchers felt thankful that they slept not in houses as do most men but in a tent. Then pipes giving out they also went to sleep and in the morning spoke of these things to the others who thereupon laughed them to scorn. Canoeists passing said they had felt nothing but a few beetles during the night. An unromantic shepherd hammered on our tent and seemed aggrieved at the use of his poles.

Loading up we cleared off after breakfast and arrived in the rain in some cul de sac. Donning macs we pulled under some trees and waited for that rain to stop. A discussion ensued as to how long water-proofs are worthy of the name, with a compulsory trial of an hour or so. Then we find we are down the wrong channel, but half an hour's pull in the rain puts <u>that</u> right, and everybody blames everybody else for taking us the wrong way. It cleared at last and getting into the proper channel we arrived at a farm where flat rocks suggested a bathe. G. suggested leapfrog and deluged us with water as his mighty form disappeared in the foaming wave. B. took a walk of several miles and the boat, relieved of his 12 stone, speeded cheerily on. Grand views of the winding stream appeared through the trees, the boat like an energetic beetle far down below.

Zig-zagerated view of the Wye.
Man in boat — 'Can't get over, can you?'
'No, shall have to go round, it's only a few miles.'

Later on a sharp turn and swift current wedged the boat's nose in some stones in the bank, she swung round to flee down-stream stern first — a lucky escape.

We run into some rocks above Foy, fortunately no damage done. It is difficult to know where to go generally and while you are thinking about it you find the boat going broadside on at the rate of ten miles an hour on to stones, or, as in this case, bow on to the bank, the current then whirling you all over the river.

G. was very justly proud of his idea for airing things, and was (very properly) photographed by H. 'But O! What a difference' when the wind blew.

It was yet early times when a tight little island hove in sight, called Foy;
we took possession by planting our colours. It was a much bepastured
spot, and disturbing horses, cows, ducks and geese we at last found a
space for camp.

For fishing H. says this beat anything he had seen so far, and comes in
with some infant salmon, eaten for breakfast next morning.

The entire occupants of a farm-house came to the door and duly gave permission to camp. Our envoy returning and reporting young women, G. discovered we wanted milk, and accompanied maiden to the hen roost etc. The contents of the boat having meanwhile been deposited in the mud, H. & Gg. engaged in fishing. A heaving struggling mass of canvas contained G., & B. dug a trench for the fire. Enters an elderly man who did not appear to have seen anything quite so wonderful as our arrangements in all his life. A small gratuity secured us against the horses, and the old man who might have been an ancient Briton retired well pleased. He had told his missis that he 'know'st they boys was up to summat'. Our piscators returned bearing finny spoil, and supper was indicated. While engaged thereon we heard voices and B. mounted guard with air gun and challenged them. They thereupon came up and derived much edification from a contemplation of our domestic arrange-ments. G. showed them the deadly nature of the gun on insects of which we had not a few, and we handed remains of our curry to a man who after tasting it, smiled sadly, and gave it to some boys who got through it safely.

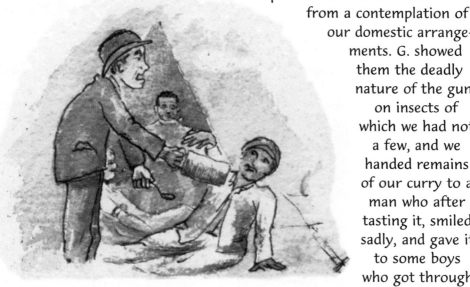

It was dark, but we accepted the man's
invite to visit the 'Hole in the Wall', and
after floundering through mud and water
found a spring. Higher up in the rocks
water could be heard trickling. The man's
household supplied us with salt for a
month. Passing a farmhouse G. saw female
shadows on the blind and returned in
ecstacy.

The man brought us a bushel of apples in
the morning after which we got away and
arrived at Ross, surveying the Prospect,
calling at the P.O., at the church, the
Town Hall and the 'Saracen's Head' (for wood carvings). B. was absurdly
proud of a white flannel cap he had purchased, and a fisherman
discoursed on salmon fishing.

Ross Town Hall

'Sologram' cut in stone in south wall of market house, Ross, supposed to signify 'Faithful to Charles in heart' and placed there by John Kyrle, The Man of Ross, 1680.

Elms growing inside Ross church. Legend relates that a vicar cut down the Man of Ross's own particular yew outside the church, whereupon two young ones sprang up through the floor and flourished inside the window to the great delight of the people. The stems now only remain, but a creeper gives to one the appearance of life.

Ancient Briton going fishing in his coracle

Goodrich Castle

Afloat again we passed Wilton Castle on the right, and arrived at Goodrich castle. A gamekeeper gave us permission to camp, (rather an ambitious project as our luggage was great and the castle up a hill some distance from the river). However a procession was formed but soon collapsed.

Goring - 'Me am almost done up quite.'

Here Gg. was prostrate, stretched like Issachar between two burdens, there B. seated on bundle of rugs mopping his perspiring brow, and then goes G. staggering under three kit bags, and a couple of Gladstones, muttering condemnatory remarks on things in general. H. was occupying himself in getting the thousand and one things out of the boat. Oars and poles were deposited in the undergrowth, and eventually everything was got up to the Castle. The custodian eyed us somewhat askance; he was used to people visiting, but here we were come evidently came to stay. We told him we had permission (without mentioning authority) and he was affability itself.

B. had been here before and asked after old man's wife, on which he burst into tears, she was 'gone'; she had told B. that 'She was as weak as a robin'. The good old man did not forget to mention as to fees, and promised to come in the morning and bring his fiddle.

More stores for the camp

Surrounded by ruined walls we pitched our tent, a fine place was found, and soon the roaring fire was boiling soup and cooking proceeded under the able hands of Gg.

We were delighted to find a fair artist at work in the central court, giving an opportunity to G. who is a great art critic to render valuable assistance.

The evening drawing on she packed up and made her way to Goodrich Court, which is on the next bend, picturesquely built overlooking the Wye.

This was the best pitch we had, free from coleoptera, diptera, etc.

Good old Gg. does the cooking and nearly roasts himself into the bargain in a very convenient corner of an old staircase. The draught was so great that very soon a pile of sticks put there by somebody was consumed. The curry formed the pièce de resistance at the Banquet.

We naturally turned to the Banqueting Hall and under a starry roof, on a table made of loose boards, we spread our dish cloth, sorry! <u>table</u>cloth, and with a lamp at each end the steaming stew did make unto ourselves an unctuous feast.

'Gadzooks' and 'Grammercy' likewise 'ods bobs' and 'byie halidom'! We are in the Middle Ages once again!
Were not the shadows on the wall those of long lost heroes? Is not that clanking sound the mailed sentry on the ramparts?
'Nay! twas but the wind
Or the tin upsetting on the raging fire
On with the feast!
Let belts be unconfined
No rest till morn, when tinned Ram we eat.'

We dine in the Banqueting Hall (rather eerie) and though we called on the scullions to clear up, there was no voice, save the bleating of sheep or the restless cry of some bird.

The fine old castle must have looked odd from the village, quite haunted with lights shining through the gaping windows. The rage of hunger now appeased, we sat round and smoked our pipes moralizing on fallen greatness and generally enjoying the reward of our excursions. No sound but the 'night winds whispering low' the ghosts of knights and ladies, the Lords of Goodrich and of that brave garrison which in King Charles' reign held out for five months against Cromwell's Roundheads, passed before us peopling the ruined courts. A chief named Godricus Dux built the castle and King John presented it to William Strigul in 1204. The keep is more ancient and was built by an Irish chieftain as ransom for his son. 'In shape the castle is a parallelogram, with round towers at its angles and is entered by a long passage divided into sections by gates and portcullis'. The visitor of obnoxious intent was received with boiling water in one, molten lead in the next, probably brick bats in another while arrows would rattle on his armour all the way. It is not a matter for surprise therefore that the castle was <u>not</u> entered by the passage but rather the Lady's Tower in the wall of which a huge gap appears.

We made for the tent, and wrapped in our rugs slept peacefully till dawn. The ruins abounded in owls chanting in crescendo, chattering jackdaws and cooing pigeons, which delightful noises ceased gradually as day drew on.

Seated on benches (a luxury for us) we breakfasted in the warm sun, H. taking snap shots.

The tent was struck and the janitor appeared shortly after. B borrowed the fiddle and played the 'pas de quatre', G. dancing and the old man striking up a waltz that became general. The old man's nieces and some girls and some visitors arrived and we scaled the walls, were shown the dungeons, and some freehand drawings by King Henry IV.

G. obliges with the 'pas de quatre' - by himself.

B. and G. waltz, 'Till they laughing, tumble flat upon the ground'.

Drawings in the castle attributed to Henry IV.

Rolling things down the slopes was easier than carrying them, oars were dragged from their hiding place, the boat loaded and we dropped down the river for a bathe. Refreshed, we rowed on until the gigantic vertical cliffs of Coldwell Rocks appeared, 600 feet high and quite chilly in the shade. Once more we glide into the sunshine.

At the New Weir B. became somewhat pensive, for was it not here that a former trip was cut short by a catastrophe to the boat which filled and sank after running on the rocks. The wreck was sent back on a donkey cart to Ross and the two occupants did a thumb to Chepstow, their destination. The sculls having become damaged B. spliced the blades with wire, and we arrived at the most picturesque part of the river—Symonds Yat (signifying the Gate of the Wye). Our boat aroused the languid interest of the watermen and we left it in their charge to climb the steep cliffs to the top of the Yat, a huge mass of carboniferous limestone. The river may be seen winding in a curve of four miles, while the distance across the Yat is a little under 600 yards. The Welsh Hills, Coldwell Rocks, Forest of Dean and many villages form a splendid panorama.

At
Symonds Yat

H. had left us at Welsh Bicknor, striking across fields for the station to get
meat and photo requisites, and seeing a train come in we could see him
sigh as he contemplated the climb in store having recognised our hand-
kerchiefs waving away up. G. held a levee of small country maidens laden
with ginger-pop, a glorious sunset giving charming tints to the hills
around.

Descending, we got afloat and paddled through darkening ravines looking in vain for a suitable camping ground. Deep pools, some 60 feet deep marks the approach to the Little Doward below which is a dangerous channel through rocks. We crept along slowly in the darkness until the sound of broken water ahead put us very much on the qui vive. Getting the boat's nose pointed for the narrow channel we let her go, and in a moment were through and poling vigorously to keep her from running into the bank. She came through very well considering the darkness. Finding a low bank on the left we stopped the boat and with all haste unloaded. G. got up the tent and a hasty meal was ready at about 10.30pm—a kind of amalgamation as we had had neither lunch, dinner, tea nor supper and now ate enough for all four; retiring soon after we slept well and woke to find the sun shining brilliantly.

A gamekeeper of cheery disposition came to see us, and made us welcome
over the adjoining demesne, his master being away from home. He said
that some fellows had pitched a tent in the neighbouring woods with
intent to live on game, but were starved out.

G. requests
Gg. to tuck in
his tuppeny

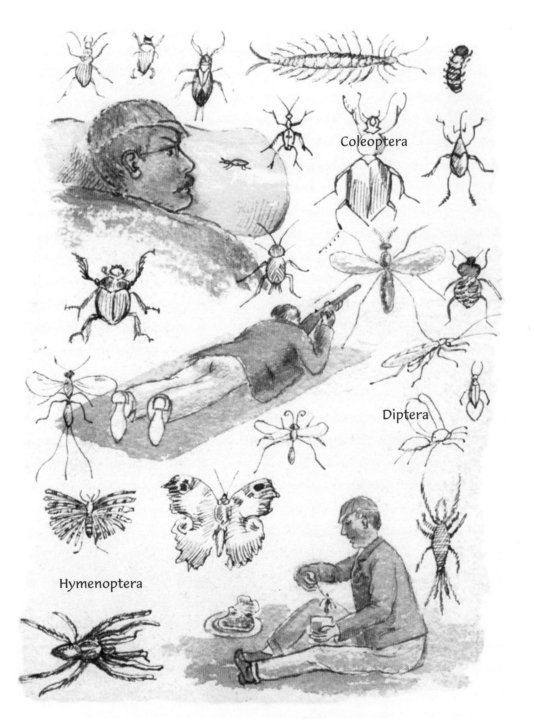

Coleoptera

Diptera

Hymenoptera

This does not do full justice to the many beautiful objects in the insect world that invaded our tent nightly on the lamp being lit. Here we see G. doing execution with his airgun, and Gg. fishing out a remarkably fine specimen of the order Diptera from the jam pot before beginning his breakfast.

Later on we crossed the river and after a steep climb found on the far side some caves—Arthur's Cave, Arthur's Hall etc.—exploring same with lantern, but finding no relics of habitation although bones of all kinds had been discovered. Those of red deer, grouse etc. were seen, and we rather ungratefully brought away a hawk's skull as a memento, found tied to a stick as a warning to others.

Discovery of mysterious lump of limestone, supposed bone of fossilis equis or fossil horse

'Here is a well preserved British Camp, with a double vallum on the N.E. and a quadrangular area open on the S.E. but otherwise defended by steep cliffs'. This is said to be a camp of Caractacus who from this place bade defiance to the Roman general, Ostorius, and had such a battle in the passage that it is called the 'Slaughter' unto this day. A well-like cavity contained a skeleton of large size and a long excavation of about a mile was used for exercising horses. A tumulus covers the remains of some long forgotten hero of whom might be written, as of a similar chieftain's grave found in Cornwall:

What noble dead lies here
Lone on this moorland drear ...
Haply is here the grave of Briton warrior brave...
Who deemed that here might fame to later years proclaim
His val'rous deeds:- but faithless to its trust
Fame hath not left the venerated dust
The shadow of a name

Caractacus
on guard at the
Little Doward

41

Ascending
a tower of
slender iron work with H. below with camera we had a fine view, and also
discovered some tokens left there by a young couple of amorous feelings.
Coming down we struck a path with sundry boughs strewn across, probably to warn carts etc. of
the presence of wire
netting enclosing young
pheasants. In the
village a travelling
bear was amusing the
youngsters. We came
across our friend the
gamekeeper and had
another chat, and discov-
ered several caverns, selecting
the most break neck routes down to
the river.

Dixton Church

42

In the afternoon we explored the fields and met a young farmer engaged in harvesting who led us to his farm through apple orchards alive with geese and turkeys. He was very hospitable and we sat in his garden and drank cyder and talked through the afternoon. His family (butterfly catching) came round to the tent, which the ladies had already inspected during our absence and had remarked that they 'thought a woman might have made the place look more comfortable'.

Playing (sic)
on the ole banjo.

We were striking tent and after adieus dropped down to Monmouth, laying up to have a broken rowlock mended, and we replenished our ale jars at an Inn. The keeper in attendance had spent a time in Edinburgh and was therefore accustomed to medical students, but fixed upon B. who is a layman as to the disciple of the healing (?)art, much flattered that two men spent the after-noon and much tin there, and was found by the party still liquidating on their return from a tour of the place. All being now safely aboard we pushed off and rowed to Bigsweir where the tide is first felt, B. & Gg. landing to tow as far as Tintern.

At the King's Head,
Monmouth.

However, masted vessels obstructed the line and B. lost the boat and went astray in a wood, afterwards finding himself in a hotel and then emerging at Tintern village; the tide had meanwhile turned and the boat came in sight, but boarding was difficult and she dropped down to a meadow below the abbey, a cheerless drizzle coming on and darkness falling. After coming across to fetch B. we were all soon busy staggering through mud and water unloading the boat.

It is a very rapid tide (at Chepstow the fall is about 40 feet) and our boat was soon left in the sludge and reeds while G. as usual, having first planted the standard, got the tent up and the baggage was transferred to its welcome cover, the canvas steaming from the heat of the lamp.

Effect of landing in the mud at Tintern

Under such circumstances tea is <u>the</u> thing. We were imbibing some when a frightful hulla-baloo proceeded from a farm somewhere near, and G. shouting in reply came in with the information that the farmer must be drunk as he could get no information to show what was wrong. We were too fagged to bother about it and went to sleep.

G. comes in and reports farmer drunk and using 'language'.
Note G.'s shocked expression

We paid a duty visit in the morning and the farmer finding we were customers, apologises, became affable and suggested his favourite ration—cyder, a handsome girl, his dark eyed daughter, bringing out a large jug of the same. He accentuated his remarks by a constant use of his fore-finger and would have the girl wash our travel stained clothes if necessary. We soon enjoyed a much needed ablution, and came away with eggs, milk and vegetables.

We avail ourselves of the farmer's hospitality

One of the crew tries to ingratiate himself with the lovely maid by a present of cornflour, onions and rice.

It was raining all day and we explored the abbey—a majestic pile. Yankees of course in evidence. G. & B. lunched at an Inn and afterwards trained to Chepstow, finding more Americans, H. & Gg. meanwhile occupying themselves in making a pudding of all the cornflour, eggs, custard powders etc. etc. in stock, proudly presenting same to the others on their return. It was voted 'off' and was made the medium of another interview with the dark eyed daughter and duly presented to her with a quantity of rice. She thought it would benefit the geese and seemed quite charmed with the gift. B. had been to the village for stores and had purchased some whiskey (for medicinal purposes). Calling at the farm on his return the farmer showed him silver prizes won at shows and the girl brought the inevitable cyder, an attention responded to by the production of the whiskey which the farmer seemed to much appreciate; the mixture however had a somnolent effect on B. who disgusted the party by snoring unbearably, until roused by boots and other moveable articles.

Farmer's daughter brings down a <u>baby</u> to the great confusion of the party. Retirement of same.

Breakfast next day was ready by 12 and dinner by 10 pm as we had got into most irregular habits; eggshells, unwashed articles thrown down anywhere and a general disinclination to amend had now settled down on the whole party. On Camping trips some order is necessary, and each man should take it in turn to set things in order, without which comfort is not possible. Of course, away from houses one is apt to be somewhat careless in this respect, but here, close to the village, mixing with people, the contrast was most striking, the Hotel people of course thinking our habits a kind of outrage on the locus standi of the place, when every other building is a place of accommodation for tourists. One landlord quite 'gave us up' apparently thinking we were neither 'feather, flesh nor good red herring',

but we drank his liquids and retired to our inexpensive if lowly couches fuelling that noble sense of independence dear to every British soul. 'Never was a more beautiful building erected on a more charming site than Tintern—it was founded by Cistercian monks in the early part of the 12th century by Walter de Clare, its history uneventful, but very brief for in 1537 it was given up into the hands of Henry VIII's Ecclesiastical commissioners and soon afterwards fell into ruins.'

'It is built of old red sandstone, cruciform in shape, the extra-
ordinary beauty of the proportions and the extreme delicacy
of the work must strike even the most casual visitor, and the
impression is heightened by the exquisite bits of landscape of
the surrounding hills that are framed within the empty
mullions of the windows.' Length 228 ft. breadth 37 ft.
transept 150 ft., height 70 ft. At back of N. transept are the
conventional buildings.

We packed up and rowed down to Chepstow passing men salmon fishing, stone quarries on the left and soon the Iron Tubular Bridge of Brunel, 600 ft. long, divided into one span of 300 ft. and three shorter spans of 100 ft. each was passed. H. was understood to say he would prepare breakfast. On our asking for it, he indicated a mug, a milk can and a loaf lying on the grass!

Brunel's Bridge, Chepstow

Broiling sun down the mouth of the river.
Exhaustion of G. and Gg.

The river widened considerably, the shores at low water looking desolate and generally unsuitable for camping. The castle at Chepstow is a mighty mass of masonry occupying nearly 4 acres on a platform of rock rising sheer from the river. It was originally built for one of the Norman Earls

of Hereford in the 11th century, and is now in the possession of the Duke of Somerset who owns more ruined castles than any individual in Great Britain. The most stirring event in its history took place in the Civil Wars, and the fortress was taken by assault by Colonel Morgan after a short siege, many of the garrison with their brave commander being cruelly murdered. Henry Martyn the regicide was here imprisoned, as also for a short time a far better man— Jeremy Taylor.

Here B. having to go North took a regretful leave. The rest of the crew dropped down to the mouth of the river, came back with the tide and pitched camp near Chepstow.

As B. has to go to Glasgow, he climbs a bank to catch the train to Chepstow

At the last camp, Chepstow, waiting for cart to take baggage to the station.

The boat was left at the landing stage in charge of Jordan's men and the remains of the stores handed over to some cottagers. A cart having been procured, the baggage was taken to the station—a little difficulty as to tickets was surmounted by leaving it in charge of the station master and the party took the train for town to once more undergo the regularity of every-day life and to look back on the contrasts afforded thereto by the incidents connected with 'Camping on the Wye'.

At Chepstow Station Messrs. H. Gg. and G. have to take tickets, and produced in bronze $2^{1}/_{2}$, a fly-book and such like valuable effects. Station master eventually issues tickets, keeping their baggage as security.

'The life is rough, but these things recommend themselves to those who, as Kinglake says: "not being born with chiffney bits in their mouths, are tired of living in a state of utter respectability, cruelly pinioned at dinner tables, or solemnly planted in pews".
'In the Forests of Brazil'
An Oxford Undergraduate